Sport Zone

CW01651713

A Crazy Sport

David Orme

Published in 2002 by:
Nelson Thornes Ltd
Delta Place
27 Bath Road
CHELTENHAM
GL53 7TH
United Kingdom

02 03 04 05 06 / 10 9 8 7 6 5 4 3 2 1

A catalogue record for this book is available from the British Library

ISBN 0-7487-6404-6

Illustrations by Zhenya Matysiak
Cover illustration by Rob Hefferan (represented by Advocate)
Page make-up by Peter Nickol

Printed and bound in Great Britain by T. J. International

Contents

Chapter 1

Warming up – for torture!

I often wonder why I ever took up this crazy sport. Swimming, cycling and running are all really hard to get right. People spend their lives working at just one. Why am I trying to be brilliant at all three? Why don't I just do one?

Why not take up something that doesn't involve swimming in freezing cold water to start with?

"Five minutes!" called Mrs Perkins. She's in charge of the event.

That was a signal for me to make sure I was warmed up. Warmed up! I imagined how it was going to feel diving into that cold water.

I knew it was going to be a tough year. I was eleven, and had become a “senior youth” triathlete. That meant I was up against people as old as fourteen. Not much chance of my winning anything.

The distances are much longer too. Last year we swam one hundred metres, biked five kilometres, and ran one kilometre. Now the

swimming distance is double, and the other distances have gone up even more.

I carried on jogging gently around the pool. For triathlons, outdoor pools are best. Adults often swim in the sea.

While I was warming up I thought about the toughest race of all, the Iron Man competition. That involves swimming nearly four kilometres, then biking for 180 kilometres, then running a

marathon! There isn't an Iron Woman competition. Just as well!

Mrs Perkins blew her whistle. Time to get out of my nice, warm tracksuit. The water looked cold! If only we were allowed to wear wetsuits!

Chapter 2

Way behind

Most of the other girls in that race were older and taller, but I knew Tina was about the same age as me. I had tried to be friendly, but she didn't seem to want to be friends with anyone. I thought she was a bit stuck up.

She was standing by the pool, jumping up and down, shaking her fingers, all that sort of thing.

I looked across. "Water looks cold!" I said.

She just nodded and carried on with her warming up exercises. Be like that then, I thought.

Bang! In we dived, into the water. Cold? No, it wasn't cold. It was absolutely freezing! I knew I'd soon be really hot, but that doesn't help when you hit the water!

Swimming isn't my strongest event. In any case, the taller girls had a big advantage.

At least in a pool you swim in lanes. Sea swimming can get quite rough. And I don't just mean the waves! People barge you out of the way, or just swim right over you.

I couldn’t get going during the first length. My turn was awful. Then things got better. I was way behind everyone else, though.

By the last length I was going really well. Then I felt a bit of cramp in my leg. It wasn’t too bad, but I hoped it wouldn’t get worse. I had a lot to do that afternoon!

Chapter 3

On your bike!

I pulled myself out of the pool a clear last. The rest of the girls were busy getting their cycling stuff on in the transition area. I couldn't see Tina – surely she wasn't on her bike already?

This is always the worst bit of the whole race. You have to pull your cycling stuff on over wet arms and legs. "No time for hair dryers and talcum powder," my junior trainer used to say.

Done! I grabbed my bike and was just about to jump on when I remembered something. Helmet! If I whizzed off without that I'd be disqualified!

I quickly put it on and set off. I was still last, of course, but I hoped I would do better now. Cycling was my strongest event.

Most triathlons use roads for the cycling section. We were just using the running track at the stadium. The danger on a narrow track is from bunching. The cycling section is the one

that causes most injuries. As I was last, bunching wasn't going to be a problem for me!

It always seems strange at first on the bike. This is because you're using different muscles. Instead of your legs going up and down, they have to start going round and round. It's hard at first.

I've got another name for the triathlon: torture!

I looked ahead. One of the older girls was slowing down. She looked as if she was in trouble. Maybe I could get past! I changed gear and really started to push. For one second I felt the cramp again, but it went away. I shot past.

I found out later that she had a problem with her bike. I had been too busy to notice!

4

Chapter 4

Run, rabbit, run

Into the transition area again. Triathlon isn't only about swimming, cycling and running. It's also about how fast you can change your clothes! Something always gets caught up and you're stuck there hopping about on one leg looking like someone in a Big Losers one-legged race.

Back on the track I went. One of the girls had had a technical problem with her running shoes, otherwise known as putting them on the wrong feet! That meant another place made up.

I'd really got a second wind now. Could I

make up another place? Maybe just one. Another girl was lagging behind. It was Anita. Her problem was too many cheeseburgers between races!

I pushed my speed up – a bit like changing gear on the bike – and set off to catch her.

I was nearly up to her when I heard a roar from across the track. Someone had won! I knew I shouldn't, but I just had to look. I knew those yellow running shorts! Tina!

Chapter 5

Saying sorry

How had Tina managed it? She must be brilliant!

I just managed to get past Anita before the finishing line. Three people behind me, and me the youngest in the race. Not too bad! And I'd really enjoyed it. I must be mad!

Then Tina came over to me.

"I want to say sorry," she said. I was amazed, and a bit puzzled.

"What for?"

"Before the race. You tried to be friendly, and I was rude. It's just…"

She stopped and sat down. I could see she was really exhausted.

"For most people, triathlon is a bit of fun at the weekend. That's fine, but it's not how I think of it. I have this special way of getting ready for a race. It's not just about exercises. It's a special way of thinking about the race,

and going through it in my mind. That's why I seemed rude."

I suddenly liked Tina.

"That's all right! So you really want to go a long way, then?"

She nodded.

"In seven years' time, I want to be picked for

the Olympics. And when I am, I want the gold medal."

I could tell she was really determined. I was sure she would make it.

* * * * *

So that's how we became friends. Tina has helped me a lot. Of course, I'll never get to the Olympics. Not as an athlete, anyway. But maybe I'll be in the crowd, cheering when they put that gold medal round Tina's neck.

Sports Zone

If you like this book, you may also enjoy others from the same series.

Up For It! (Football)
Trail Bikes (Mountain biking)
Snow Trek (Snowboarding)
Hot Skates (Ice hockey)
Head to Head (Sprint relay)
A Crazy Sport (Triathlon)

Rock Face (Rock climbing)
Speed Bikes (Speedway)
Running into Trouble (Marathon)
Skating to Danger (Outdoor skating)
Hit It! (Water skiing)
Goalie's Nightmare (Football)

Match Ref (Football – coaching, refereeing)
Dive and Survive (Sea diving)
Pit Stop (Formula 1)
Deep Trouble (Potholing)
In at the Deep End (Swimming)
Close to the Wind (Windsurfing)